EARTH ROCKS

SOIL

Richard Spilsbury

WAYLAND

First published in Great Britain in 2016 by Wayland

Editors: Sarah Eason and Tim Cooke
Cover design: Lisa Peacock

Produced for Wayland by Calcium

ISBN: 978 1 5263 0201 4
10 9 8 7 6 5 4 3 2 1

Wayland
An imprint of
Hachette Children's Group
Part of Hodder & Stoughton
Carmelite House
50 Victoria Embankment
London EC4Y 0DZ

An Hachette UK Company
www.hachette.co.uk

www.hachettechildrens.co.uk

Picture acknowledgements:

Key: b=bottom, t=top, r=right, l=left, m=middle, bgd=background

Picture credits: Cover: Dreamstime: Jon Helgason; Inside: Dreamstime: Antonialorenzo 8–9, Celia Maria Ribeiro Ascenso 12–13, Michal Bednarek 20–21, Javarman 20, Attila Németh, 13t, Edward Westmacott 24–25; Shutterstock: Africa Studio 15b, James Chen 6–7t, Chromatika Multimedia snc 14, Coprid 13bl, FocalPoint 13br, Warren Goldswain 11b, Eric Isselee 17, Paul Maguire 16, Melkor3D 4, motorolka 15t, Christian Musat 27t, Ozja 21, photka 27b, Patrick Poendl 25tr, Sapsiwai 6–7b, SeDmi 23, smereka 22, snapgalleria 19, think4photop 26, TsuneoMP 4–5, violetkaipa 1, 11t, xpixel 5, Yojik 10; Wikimedia Commons: Grönneger 1 18.

CONTENTS

Secret Soil...4

From Rocks to Soil 6

Moving Rocks......................................8

Sudden Soils 10

Plants in Soil....................................12

Recyclers 14

Animals in Soil 16

Different Soils 18

Soils Around the World....................20

Using Soil..22

Spoiling Soil.....................................24

Super Soil 26

Rock Your World! 28

Glossary 30

Further Reading................................31

Index 32

SECRET SOIL

Most people do not even think about the soil beneath their feet. They walk around on it, play ball on it, maybe even dig and grow plants in it, but they do not stop to think about the secrets in the soil. To them, and perhaps to you, soil is just dirt. Think again! Soil is a living system.

A LIVING THING

The layer of earth that covers much of the planet is made up of a whole variety of things, including pieces of rock that might have been formed by **volcanoes**, decaying plants and animals and their waste, air, and water and millions of living things.

Volcano

Clues to the Past

The contents of an area of soil tell us a lot about its history. Soil can tell us what the weather was like in the past, what animals and plants lived and grew there and how much water covered the land long ago.

Bacteria are just one of the living things in soil. A lump of soil the size of a pencil rubber may have more than 2.5 billion bacteria in it. There will be thousands of different types of bacteria in it, too. That is why you should always wash your hands after touching soil.

ROCK STAR STORIES

The remains of sabre-toothed tigers found in soil tell us that these huge killer cats roamed the Earth thousands of years ago.

SOIL POWER

Almost everything that we need can be traced back to soil: food, clothing, paper, wood and even the air we breathe. We depend on soil to grow food and to hold up our buildings. Soil is an amazing resource, and our lives would not be the same without it. Read on and you will never think soil is dull again!

FROM ROCKS TO SOIL

Half of soil is air and water. Tiny grains of rock are one of the next most important ingredients. However, most rocks we see range from beach pebbles to cliff faces and high mountains. How do the grains of rock in soil get to be so small?

ATTACKED BY THE ELEMENTS

The rocks on the Earth's surface are constantly being broken down by wind, water and ice. Wind can toss grains of sand against a rock and wear away its surface. Water in a river can scrape boulders across a rock's surface and break off chunks. Rainwater contains **acids** that can wear away rock, too.

Powerful ocean waves break down coastal cliffs.

FREEZE-THAW

The wearing away of rocks is called **weathering**, and it can turn even very hard rocks, such as granite, to dust. If water gets into a tiny crack in the rock and then expands (takes up more space) as it turns into ice, it forces the crack open. As this happens again and again, the crack grows bigger and bigger until the rock splits. The smaller pieces then break down further to produce soil.

Centuries of freezing then thawing change the tiniest crack into a massive split in rocks.

Clues to the Past

Sea stacks are vertical columns of rock found along rocky coasts. They are the result of ocean forces. Waves gradually change a small crack in a chunk of protruding rock into a cave. Eventually the cave roof becomes so thin it collapses, leaving a separate stack standing in the ocean.

MOVING ROCKS

In some cases soil develops directly from the rock that lies beneath it. Often, however, there is a mysterious mix of different types of rocks in soil. Sometimes, soil contains grains from a type of rock that is not found anywhere near it. How does this happen?

EROSION

The grains of rock that form soils can be moved vast distances. **Erosion** is when pieces of rock that have been worn away by weathering are carried to new places. Small pieces of lightweight rock can be blown a long way by winds. You can see this happening if you stand on a beach on a windy day and watch the grains of sand being blown by the wind.

Over thousands of years, nature can carve some remarkable shapes through weathering and erosion. These forces made the sandstone arches, pillars and other amazing landforms in places such as Arches National Park in Utah.

WATER POWER

Water is a powerful force of nature. Rivers can cross entire continents and carry rocks extremely long distances. Fast-flowing rivers can transport large rocks, but slow-moving rivers mainly transport tiny pieces of rock. Grains of rock can also be washed somewhere new by heavy rainstorms or floods.

Fast rivers carry small stones that crash into and break up larger stones.

SUDDEN SOILS

Most soils take hundreds of years to form, or even longer. Some soils have more dramatic beginnings. They form suddenly following **landslides,** volcanoes or heavy storms.

LOOK OUT, LANDSLIDE!

A landslide or mudflow is when a lot of **sediment** moves suddenly downhill. This often happens after rainstorms. Mountains have sloping sides, so when the loose rock and soils on the sides become wet and heavy, they can suddenly become unstable. They can build up a lot of speed, run off the mountain slope and form a layer of soil in a new area of flat land below.

This area of soil beneath a forest slid down when it was wet.

ROCK STAR STORIES

Plants grow rapidly in rich volcanic soil.

Have you ever asked yourself why people live near volcanoes when these explosive giants can be so dangerous? It is because the volcanic soil around them is so good for growing crops. Volcanic ash is rich in **nutrients** that plants take in through their roots to help them to grow.

ERUPTIONS

A volcanic eruption can change the soil in an area dramatically. When a volcano erupts, it rains volcanic ash down onto the Earth's surface. This ash mixes with other grains of rock to form a rich, dark soil.

erupting volcano

PLANTS IN SOIL

Plants do not just grow in soil. They are living things that form an important part of the complex world of the soil. Plants make soil a living, breathing thing!

THE ROLE OF ROOTS

When plants grow in soil, their roots stretch between and around the tiny grains of rock within it. The plant uses its roots to anchor itself in the ground so it can grow tall. However, acids released by the roots of some plants break down the rock on which the soil is forming. Roots also help to bind together the grains of rock in newly-formed soil. As the roots grow and tunnel through the soil, they open up spaces to let in the air and water that make up soil.

Plant root tips force their way between rock grains in soil to reach water and nutrients.

PLANT POWER

Plants are unique. They are the only living things that make their own food using the power of sunlight. They use **carbon dioxide** from the air and water from the soil to make sugars that help them to grow stems, leaves, flowers, fruits and seeds. When plant parts drop off or plants die, they decay and release their stored nutrients into the soil, enriching the soil itself.

Energy from the sun helps plants to make food.

ROCK STAR STORIES

Plants can even help to break up rocks into smaller grains that make up soil. When plants start to grow in a crack in a rock, their roots widen the crack as they expand and spread, eventually breaking the rock apart.

This plant is growing through a crack in the rock.

RECYCLERS

Many of the organisms in soil are so small that we can only see them with a microscope, but they do a big job. These **microorganisms** are nature's recyclers. They break down plant and animal waste into substances that help to make soil the remarkably useful resource that it is.

SOIL WORKERS

Living microorganisms, such as tiny creatures called mites, bacteria and **fungi** such as mushrooms, are a vital ingredient of soil. These **decomposers** feed on **organic** waste such as leaves and animal dung. As they do so, they release nutrients into the soil. These nutrients form a dark, spongy substance called **humus**. Humus helps to bind tiny grains of rock together and helps soil to store water.

One thousand bacteria could fit on the head of one pin, but they do a huge job by making soil fertile and clearing up waste.

earthworm

Earthworms are soil heroes! They bring organic matter down from the **topsoil** and mix it with the soil below. Their tunnels let in air and water that bacteria and other microorganisms need to survive. Earthworms also make soil **fertiliser**. They eat soil and as it passes out of their bodies it forms worm-shaped coils of dirt called casts. These casts contain important soil nutrients.

ROCK STAR STORIES

fungus

Clues to the Past

Flowering plants make tiny pollen grains that help them to make seeds. In some soils, the tough outer coat of a pollen grain can survive long after the plant has rotted away. Scientists can examine the pollen in these soils to discover when it was alive and what type of plants grew there at that time.

ANIMALS IN SOIL

Many larger animals live in soil, too. Rabbit, badgers, mice and other animals find shelter underground or feed on roots or smaller animals in soil. They also help create soil and keep it healthy.

Up to 22.5 tonnes of animal life can live in a single hectare of soil.

THE BURROWERS

Ants, rabbits, prairie dogs and many other animals dig burrows into soil. Moles have shovel-shaped front feet with tough, wide claws to help them dig efficiently. As these animals dig their tunnels, they loosen and mix the soil. This helps to spread organic matter and **minerals** throughout the soil. It also lets in more air and water.

FEEDING THE SOIL

Waste from animals and their activities add nutrients to the soil. For example, mice carry seeds and other plant materials into their underground burrows to put into food stores and to make bedding. This material gradually decays and becomes part of the soil.

ROCK STAR STORIES

Prairie dogs dig huge networks of tunnels in soil. Prairie dogs are often accused of damaging farm machinery or injuring cattle because of their burrows, and are blamed for eating and damaging crops. In fact, these furry creatures are soil heroes! As well as making burrows that let in air and mix soil, prairie dogs eat a lot of plants. This stops the surface from becoming overgrown and allows a wide variety of plants to thrive at the surface. As a result, a wider range of nutrients from plant waste is added to the soil.

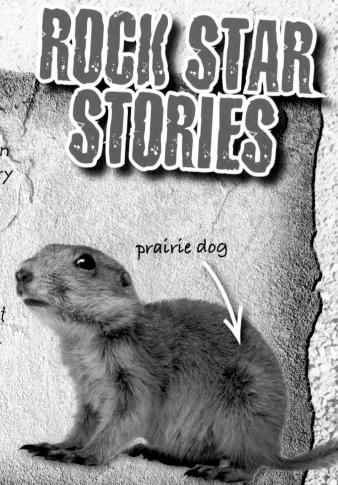

prairie dog

DIFFERENT SOILS

Soils have similar basic ingredients, but there are many different types of soils. Scientists have identified more than 70,000 kinds of soils in the United States alone. The mystery is all in the mix.

MIX IT UP!

Soils can be black, brown, grey, red or yellow. They can be crumbly, soft or grainy. Soils look different depending on their particular make-up. Red soils contain more iron minerals and dark soils are rich in humus. Soils that contain harder minerals may have larger rock grains and be more gravelly. Clay minerals soak up water, so clay soils feel stickier.

the peat bog man

Clues to the Past

The body of a man who died 2,500 years ago was discovered in a bog in Denmark in 1950. Boggy soils contain few decomposers to rot a body, so we can see exactly how the man would have looked when he died thousands of years ago. We would not know about the peat-bog man were it not for the boggy soil he died in.

There are four main layers in most soils. The depth and ingredients in each layer can vary.

Topsoil: Upper layer made up of minerals and living and rotting materials such as leaves, plants and worms. It contains a lot of humus, so it usually looks dark.

Subsoil: This layer contains less organic matter than topsoil and more minerals. It is usually lighter in colour.

Weathering horizon: This layer is made up of small pieces of rock and a very small quantity of organic matter.

Bedrock: The solid layer of rock that forms the base or bed of the soil.

topsoil

subsoil

weathering horizon

bedrock

This illustration shows the four main layers in soil.

SOILS AROUND THE WORLD

There are different types of soils around the world. They range from the dry sandy soils of hot deserts to the frozen **permafrost** soils of the far north.

DESERT SOILS

The **climate** of a region is an important factor in the types of soils found there. Climate is the typical weather patterns in a wide area. Desert soils are shallow and dry because they form in arid (very dry) climates. Soil formation is usually limited to near the surface. Water does not move through the soil, and the lack of water means there are few plants.

dry, cracked soil

This tropical soil contains iron. It is red because it has rusted!

Woolly mammoths have been found perfectly preserved in Siberian permafrost, as though stored in a deep freeze. These remains tell us that a mammoth had a thick coat of dark brown hair up to 1 metre long. Its trunk ended in two finger-like shapes which helped it to pluck grass.

woolly mammoth

COLD AND HOT

Around the Poles and on high mountains, the subsoil can remain permanently frozen and is known as permafrost. In warm regions that get plenty of rain, organic matter rots more quickly, and deep, rich tropical soils are able to form.

USING SOIL

You will be amazed by all the things soil does for us. After reading about the many uses of soil, you will never take the dirt under your feet for granted again!

Grass grows in rich, healthy soil. The grass is eaten by cows. We use cows for milk and meat.

SOIL FOR LIFE

We use soil with clay particles in it to make bricks for buildings. We need soil to grow plants, and we use plants in countless ways. Plants provide us with food, from fruit juices to the wheat that makes pizza dough, and to feed the animals we eat. We cut down trees and use the wood for fuel, furniture, building and even making paper. Plants also make the air healthier. Plants clean the air by taking out carbon dioxide and converting it to **oxygen**, which animals need to breathe.

WATER WONDER

Soil collects and stores a lot of the water that we need for drinking, washing, cleaning and cooking. As water passes through soil and flows into rivers and lakes, the soil filters out some of the **pollutants** in it, making it cleaner for us to use.

Without soil, we would live in a world of waste! Waste buried in **landfill** sites is broken down by the decomposers that live in soil. Unfortunately, plastic, glass, metal and other non-organic waste cannot be broken down like this. That is why it is best to reuse or recycle these kinds of waste if you can.

plastic bottles

ROCK STAR STORIES

SPOILING SOIL

Some soils are in danger of being spoiled by human actions. Once soil is damaged, it can be extremely difficult, if not impossible, to restore.

FARMING FEARS

Overusing or mistreating soils can ruin them. When people cut down all the trees in an area, there are no roots to hold the soil together. The wind and rain can blow and wash the valuable topsoil away. When too many animals graze an area for too long, they strip it of its plant cover and the same loss of topsoil results.

SOIL IN TROUBLE

People also spoil soil when they remove too much water from below ground for factories or other uses. This leaves the soil dry. In some places, heavy machinery can compact (squash) soil. This reduces the space available for air and water that the living things in soil, and therefore the soil itself, need to survive. Overuse of artificial **insecticides** and other farm sprays can also lower the number of decomposers in the soil, which reduces the number of nutrients and humus in it.

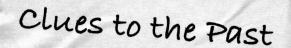

Clues to the Past

By comparing the Sahara Desert as it was in the past with how it is today, experts believe that the loss of topsoil around its edges is allowing this desert to spread at a rate of around 48 kilometres every year!

Sahara Desert

Two-thirds of the soil across the world has been spoiled to some degree by human activities, such as livestock farming.

SUPER SOIL

Soil is a vital resource for us and our planet, but it takes 500 years to develop just half a teaspoon of rich soil that is good for growing plants. That is why it is important to protect and preserve soil.

STOP SOIL EROSION

To stop the precious layer of topsoil becoming dry and washing or blowing away, people grow new plants to cover the land. Trees block the wind and plant roots bind the soil together. When there are more plants, more water soaks into the soil, helping to keep it moist.

FARMING SOLUTIONS

More and more farmers work in ways that keep soil healthy. For example, they use fewer artificial chemicals on their fields to increase the number of decomposers. They grow plants that attract insects and other animals that eat crop pests, so they do not have to use as many insecticides.

People plant trees to save soils and improve farming.

They reduce the number of times they plough a field in a year to stop the soil becoming compacted. Caring for the soil should help it provide us with food for many years to come.

Ladybird larvae hunt crop pests called aphids.

Composting is soil's super-helper. **Compost** is a dark, crumbly soil-like material made from rotted food and garden waste. Farmers and gardeners use compost as a natural fertiliser to enrich soils for future harvests. Making compost reduces the amount of rubbish we send to landfills.

ROCK STAR STORIES

food waste for compost

ROCK YOUR WORLD!

You do not have to dig deep down into the ground to see soil layers. You can make your own soil profile in an old jam jar!

YOU WILL NEED:
◇ clean, clear jar, with a lid
◇ soil
◇ water

COMPLETE THESE STEPS:

1. Fill a clean, straight-sided jar about one-third of the way up with soil.

2. Pour clean water into the jar until the jar is almost full. Watch the mixture. Can you see air bubbles rise up?

3. Now, put the lid on tightly and shake the contents of the jar. Then leave it to stand for around three hours.

4. As the water settles, different layers should appear, like a soil profile!

WHAT HAPPENED?

Pebbles and sand grains are the biggest and heaviest particles in most soils, so they form the bottom layer. The next layer up is the silt layer, because silt particles are smaller and lighter than sand. If your soil has clay in it, clay particles will be on top as they are tiny. If the soil contains very thick clay, however, there may be lumps of heavy clay at the bottom. Near the top, there will be a layer of discoloured water. This contains rotted organic matter that has dissolved in the water. At the very top there may be floating organic material that has not yet fully rotted.

discoloured water

clay

silt

pebble and
sand grains

TRY IT OUT!

Try this experiment with soils from different areas and compare the results to see how soils vary. You could also try it with soils from garden centres to see how they differ from garden soil.

GLOSSARY

acids Strong substances that can damage things.

bacteria Microscopic living things found in air, water, soil, food and even us! Some are useful; others can cause disease.

carbon dioxide A gas in the air.

climate The usual weather patterns found in a particular area.

compost A mixture of decaying vegetation and manure that can be used as a fertiliser.

decomposers Organisms that break down dead plant or animal matter.

erosion When pieces of rocks are carried somewhere new by water or wind.

fertiliser A substance that is used to make soil more suitable for growing plants.

fungi Living things such as mushrooms that usually grow in soil and feed on rotting matter.

humus A dark material in soil made from rotted plant and animal waste.

insecticides Sprays farmers use to kill insect pests.

landfill A big hole in the ground where rubbish is buried.

landslides When rocks or soil slide suddenly down the sides of hills or mountains.

microorganisms Living things so small they can only be seen through a microscope.

minerals Non-living substances that are naturally found on the Earth.

nutrients Chemicals that plants and animals need to grow and survive.

organic Produced by or from living things.

oxygen A gas in the air that animals need to breathe in order to survive.

permafrost A soil that is always frozen.

pollutants Substances that make water, soil and the air dirty or poisonous.

sediment Solid but tiny grains of matter, such as sand or silt.

topsoil The top layer of soil.

volcanoes An opening in the Earth where hot melted rock from inside the planet bursts out.

weathering The wearing away of rock and other substances by wind, water and ice.

FURTHER READING

BOOKS

Graham, Ian, *You Wouldn't Want to Live Without Soil*, Book House, 2016

Green, Jen, *Rocks and Soil* (Our Earth), Wayland, 2011

Harman, Alice, *Rocks and Soil* (Popcorn: Science Corner), Wayland, 2014

Riley, Peter, *Rocks and Soil* (Moving Up With Science), Franklin Watts, 2015

WEBSITES

Learn all about soil, play soil themed games and more at:
www.soil-net.com/primary

Would you like to hear a soil scientist talk about soil?
Then watch the video at:
www.bbc.co.uk/education/clips/z7rb4wx

Test your knowledge of different soils around the world:
http://forces.si.edu/soils/swf/whereintheworld.html

INDEX

A
animals 4, 14, 15, 16, 17, 21, 22, 24, 26, 27

B
bacteria 5, 14, 15

C
climate 20
compost 27

D
decomposers 14, 18, 23, 24, 26

E
earthworms 15
erosion 8, 9, 26

F
farming 17, 24, 26, 27
fertiliser 15, 27
freeze-thaw 7

H
humus 14, 18, 19, 24

I
insecticides 24, 26

L
landslides 10

M
microorganisms 14, 15
minerals 17, 18
mountains 6, 10, 21

N
nutrients 13, 14, 15, 17, 24

P
peat 18
permafrost 20, 21
plants 4, 11, 12, 13, 14, 15, 17, 19, 20, 22, 23, 24, 26, 27
pollutants 23

R
rivers 6, 9, 23
roots 11, 12, 13, 16, 24, 26

S
subsoil 19, 21

T
topsoil 15, 19, 24, 25, 26

V
volcanoes 4, 10, 11

W
water 4, 6, 7, 9, 12, 13, 14, 15, 17, 17, 18, 20, 23, 24, 26
weathering 7, 8, 9, 19

EARTH ROCKS

Titles in the Series

CRYSTALS

978 1 5263 0203 8

Crystals
From the Deep
Solutions
Cave Crystals
Crystal Shape
Crystal Colour and Strength
Finding Earth's Crystals
Mining Crystals
Important Crystals
Precious Stones
Crystals on Demand
Crystals in Crisis
Rock Your World!

IGNEOUS ROCKS

978 1 5263 0205 2

Igneous Rocks
Rocks From Beneath
Birth of Gemstones
Surfacing Rocks
Violent Volcanoes!
Explosive Rocks
Igneous World
Getting Igneous Rocks
Tough Rocks
Versatile Volcanics
Living by Volcanoes
Incredible Igneous
Rock Your World!

METAMORPHIC ROCKS

978 1 5263 0207 6

Metamorphic Rock
Shifting Earth
Underground Rock Factory
Pressure Points
Hot Water
Slate
Marble
Gneiss
Minerals
Reaching the Surface
Metamorphic Worldwide
Amazing Metamorphic
Rock Your World!

MINERALS

978 1 5263 0209 0

Minerals
Rock Minerals
Making Minerals
Space and Water
Recycled Minerals
Types of Minerals
Around the World
Mining Minerals
Useful Minerals
Living Minerals
Mighty Metals
Minerals Matter
Rock Your World!

SEDIMENTARY ROCKS

978 1 5263 0 1994

Sedimentary Rock
Sediments on the Move
Laying Down Layers
The Grand Canyon
Fossils in the Rock
Conglomerates
Sandstone
Mudstone
Limestone
Underground Worlds
Sedimentary Power
Super Sedimentary
Rock Your World!

SOIL

978 1 5263 0 2014

Secret Soil
From Rocks to Soil
Moving Rocks
Sudden Soils
Plants in Soil
Recyclers
Animals in Soil
Different Soils
Soils Around the World
Using Soil
Spoiling Soil
Super Soil
Rock Your World!

WAYLAND
www.waylandbooks.co.uk